A LAST LOOK AT INNOCENCE

A LAST LOOK AT INNOCENCE

◆

Middle School Kids Share Their Views of the World

Donna Silva Perry

iUniverse, Inc.
New York Lincoln Shanghai

A LAST LOOK AT INNOCENCE
Middle School Kids Share Their Views of the World

iUniverse books may be ordered through booksellers or by contacting:

iUniverse
2021 Pine Lake Road, Suite 100
Lincoln, NE 68512
www.iuniverse.com
1-800-Authors (1-800-288-4677)

ISBN-13: 978-0-595-36898-3 (pbk)
ISBN-13: 978-0-595-81719-1 (cloth)
ISBN-13: 978-0-595-81310-0 (ebk)
ISBN-10: 0-595-36898-0 (pbk)
ISBN-10: 0-595-81719-X (cloth)
ISBN-10: 0-595-81310-0 (ebk)

Printed in the United States of America

To Amanda, Jennifer and Gary; Eddie Jay, Casey, David, Gabby and Angelica; John, Marisol, and all of the children who walked through my classroom door and left me a little wiser.

Contents

THREE

SO MANY EMOTIONS

FOUR

MY REGRETS

FIVE

AMBITIONS

Preface

As a junior high guidance teacher, I have had the pleasure of sharing my classroom with adolescents for the last twenty years. It took some time for me to realize how many valuable lessons these young people were teaching me.

I learned that they were rarely disagreeable. If it seemed they were, on second look it was usually I who was off-center and in need of an attitude adjustment. If they asked me a question, I learned it was my responsibility to give them a truthful answer. I learned that the affirmations I wrote on the board for them each day were words I needed to hear. I learned that listening and hearing were separate skills. I learned patience and the importance of being truly present. I learned that if I treated them with respect, not allowing myself to make judgments, that they treated me with respect—so simple.

My students came to me with their joy, pain, peer pressure, expectations, rejections, first crushes, raging hormones, confusion, turbulent homes, identity crises, language barriers, threats from bullies, grief for deceased relatives and pets, image and appearance concerns (too tall, too short, new haircuts), anger, disappointments, dreams, and countless other issues that would bring grown people to their knees.

Day after day, they sat in their seats when the bell rang and looked at me expectantly. All that they brought with them filled me with an overwhelming sense of responsibility to be someone they could trust and someone who cared about them 100 percent. I never took their gifts of trust and caring lightly.

So, in short, this is a book about adolescence. It is a compilation of responses collected from a lesson I teach called "Sentence Completion," a kick-off exercise I give every new group of students who enter my classroom. On each sentence-completion topic, I have separated boys' responses from the girls'. Their answers can provide you with a window into the thoughts and feelings of your children, grandchildren, foster children, nieces and nephews, friends, and siblings. These are the words from those "weird" youngsters that you may consider to be anything but sensitive.

Where were you at eleven, twelve, thirteen, or fourteen? I'll remind you. It's likely you were in the same place with many of the same feelings. Even though you may have been called stupid or worse, you squared your shoulders each day and went off to school. Did you hear, "Wipe that look off your face," "You'll never amount to anything," "Don't you ever think of anyone but yourself?" or "I wish you'd never been born"? Or were you one of the lucky ones who heard "Would you like to talk about it?" "You're such a big help to me," "We're so proud of you," and "We love you no matter what"?

The process of personal growth can be daunting, and in that spirit, these pages are offered as a means to enlighten, encourage and support. As you peer into the minds of the sometimes green-haired, nose-pierced, cell-phone-addicted, seemingly hard of hearing, but totally human young people, complete the sentences yourself. I think you will find the distance between your feelings and theirs to be very narrow. Compassion, my friends, is the very least we can offer them as a gift to carry into their future.

Introduction

It is natural, as you read each fragment, to complete it with your own thoughts, and I hope you do. I suggest to my students that they not write the first response that comes to mind but rather go a little deeper and really give their answers some consideration. They are allowed more than one day to turn in their papers if they are really into it and don't want to hurry. The work is not shared in class. I make a few comments on each paper and grade it loosely by the energy they put into it. They are told that it is an opportunity to express their feelings, and, for many of them, this is a new concept. Students are also allowed to leave one or two fragments unanswered, if the thought makes them too uncomfortable. I may discuss these with them privately at a later date.

Following each topic are thought-provoking exercises. These exercises are for you, dear reader, should you choose to examine your own feelings and perhaps discover why you would respond in a certain way to the preceding sentence fragment. Maybe you've been holding on to some hurt or anger around a particular concept. Putting the emotion down on paper may help you see that it is no longer justified and that now may be the time to rethink the situation. That bag of old resentment and pain can get heavy, and it can certainly interfere with going forward in your life. Completing the exercises may also bring to your mind a particularly happy time or remind you of past successes. Perhaps you'll remember a time you left your comfort zone or took a leap of faith, discovering a strong, adventurous part of yourself you weren't aware of.

If you do choose to respond to the exercises, do not worry about format, spelling, or punctuation. Just free-writing may be best. I will not be peering over your shoulder to correct your errors.

Another goal in completing the exercises is to discover where you may have some feelings in common with the youngster in your life. You may find that you had the same concern about a certain subject when you were his or her age. This could lead you to a better understanding of where the young person is coming from. That knowledge may provide a platform for discussion rather than debate (or eye rolling, door slamming, and heavy sighing). I wish you wisdom and patience.

One

The People in My Life

Girls...

Boys replied

...are one of my best hobbies sometimes.

...are weird.

...travel in large groups.

...can drive me crazy sometimes.

...love me.

...hate me.

...aren't always my first choice.

...are the reason I go to school.

...are more open than boys.

Girls replied

...are more sensible.

...are funny when they try to act like mature women.

...tend to be too stressed out with their looks.

…always think they have to be in love when they have *no* idea what love is all about.

…sometimes ditch their best friend if the popular girls don't like her.

…follow you around with their friends and stare at you—it's scary.

…are usually too insecure to try something new, like stand out, but sometimes when they do, all of a sudden they're popular and cool—but it's risky.

GIRLS

Exercise:

1. If you are female, write about why you enjoy being female. What don't you like? How did you feel about your mother when you were young? When did you stop calling yourself a girl and start referring to yourself as a woman? Write down your thoughts.

2. If you are a male, how did you feel about your mother while growing up? Did you view her as weak or strong? Was she loving and supportive or emotionally unavailable? How do you think your relationship with your mother affects the way you relate to the women in your life today?

Boys...

Boys replied

...are weird.

...are easier to raise.

...are more scared about growing up than they would ever admit.

...are usually nicer to girls when there are no guys around.

...can be really mean to girls who aren't popular.

...tease boys that hang out with girls (but I think they're jealous).

Girls replied

...are OK, but sometimes they're disgusting.

...get in trouble more.

...always keep their feelings in.

...can be pretty immature, but good friends.

...are brats.

…are soooo cute…well, most of them.

…can make life hard for us girls.

…are more trouble than they're worth.

…try to kiss you, and if you let them they try to stick their tongue down your throat—it's *disgusting*.

BOYS

Exercise:

1. If you're a female, describe how you feel about your father. Do your feelings about him today differ from how you thought about him as a young girl? Did you ever wish you were a boy instead of a girl? Express your thoughts on these ideas.

2. If you're a male, is there someone you have thought of as a role model? What is it about him that you admire? Did you get along with your father? Do you feel you've lived up to his expectations for you? If you're a father, is there something you are consciously doing differently in raising your own children? Write about any thoughts that come to you.

Other boys and girls...

Boys

...need to learn more respect for others.

...are a bit weird—even I'm weird.

...think I'm a very cool person.

...are sometimes cruel and unforgiving.

...are cool in their own way, and I'm cool in mine.

...think I'm too nice.

...are OK, as long as they make the right decisions.

...think they know so much about life—hah!

...pretend like they can't wait to grow up, but they are really scared of the future.

Girls

...shouldn't be so judgmental of others.

...hate broccoli, but I love it.

…like me for who I am, not how I look.

…can do anything they put their minds to.

…hate me and use me.

…are too immature and don't see that their puberty problems are nothing. Problems later on are what you worry about, or problems that last forever and can't be fixed. Breakups and acne aren't problems. Problems that matter are divorce, drug addiction, alcoholism, and child abuse.

…have different talents and opinions than I do.

…think only about being popular.

…are snobby, but I can deal with it.

…are welcome to be my friends.

OTHER BOYS AND GIRLS

Exercise:

1. Was there a comment about other boys and girls that you could relate to? Tell why that phrase stood out for you.

2. Did you feel you fit in with other boys and girls when you were growing up? Write about how that perception of your childhood, positive or negative, may affect your actions and interactions as an adult.

My Mother and Father...

Boys

...are very proud of me for maintaining my grades.

...aren't married.

...are an important part of my life.

...are divorced but still love me.

...really don't get along well—my dad irritates my mom.

...worry about me a lot, and I wish they would loosen up and give me a chance to see if I'm responsible.

...well, my mother is very caring and beautiful like a monarch butterfly, and I love her.

Girls

...work a lot and come home late, and my little brother and I have to be responsible for ourselves.

...are my best friends. They have always been there for me, and I wouldn't change them for anything.

...are the most important people in my life.

...are loving, caring, and understanding.

...are strict, but I know it's for my own good.

...always yell at me. My mom complains about the way I talk to her, and every time I see my father, he yells about my being bad. No one in my family can just...*talk*!

...have very strong wills and argue often because of their stubbornness.

...have a heavy load on their shoulders, and sometimes I don't help the situation.

...are liars! They promised they wouldn't get divorced. Did they keep that promise? I don't think so!

...are pretty young for their age.

...are my main friends and have high expectations for me.

MY MOTHER AND FATHER

Exercise:

What was it like growing up in your family? Give some thought to the following questions and write about any feelings that come to you.

1. Did your mother and father spend much time with you, or did you feel they were usually too busy with work or other things that consumed their time and energy?

2. Are there family traditions that you have re-created with your own family?

3. Did your parents get divorced? Was the situation ever discussed or explained, so you weren't left feeling like the breakup was your fault? If you were old enough, were living arrangements discussed with you? Did they ask for your input?

4. If they were divorced, did they remain civil to one another, both in front of you and behind the other's back? Or did you feel like a pawn?

5. If you were angry about the way either or both of your parents treated you, have you been able to forgive them? Have you come to a place of acceptance where you truly believe they did the best they knew how? Have you considered the kind of role models *they* grew up with?

6. Did your mother and father praise and encourage you, creating the confidence that you could succeed at most any goal you set?

7. Is there something you have always wanted to say to your parents but were afraid to or did not take the time?

8. Do you have any favorite memories of your childhood that bring a smile to your face and heart?

9. Does the way you were raised affect how you are raising or raised your own children?

10. Do you feel that your mother and father were good role models?

My friends think...

Boys

...too many negative thoughts about themselves.

...that I'm a nice, honest guy to have for a friend.

...I don't know what my friends think, but I hope it's good.

...that I can be annoying.

...that I'm a funny but weird guy, but hey, I can be very original.

...I'm a smart and nice person who puts others before myself.

...I'm a bad person just because of how I dress.

...I'm a smart kid, but I don't use my intelligence in good ways.

...it's fun to use me to get what they want and then never speak to me again.

Girls

...a lot about being judged.

...that I think too much about guys and makeup.

…that I'm a good listener and problem solver.

…wrong about me.

…I'm too sensitive.

…I'm nice because I never talk behind people's backs.

MY FRIENDS THINK

Exercise:

Do most of your friends and coworkers tend to have positive views of life? Do they think there are at least as many good things happening in the world as bad? When you get together, does the conversation revolve around their successes, the grandkids, a trip they're excited about taking, improvements they've made in their homes, a good book or movie, or other pleasant conversation? Do your friends ask about you and find time to listen if you want their input on something of concern? Do they encourage you and offer to help before you even have to ask?

Maybe you have a particular friend you've been loyal to, in spite of that person's negativity. You certainly want to be supportive of friends who may be going through difficult times, but some people have victim attitudes and refuse to or cannot look on the brighter side of an issue or to seek help if that's what's needed. It's easy to feel guilty about avoiding these people, but if they are draining your energy, it may be time to let them sink or swim. They *do* have a choice…and so do you!

Two

My Personal Thoughts

Sometimes I think…

Boys

…that I will be rich.

…that no one likes me—not even my parents.

…that I should lie so I don't get in trouble.

…that my life has ended and there is no reason for me to be living because I have led a bad life.

…that people could be nice if they chose to.

…about world chaos.

…that I haven't lived much and I should try more things.

…life is very complicated.

…about retiring.

…that the world is like a big soccer ball and if you kick it hard it will explode, but if you kick it softly it will float like a feather and make a goal.

…bullies use me as their chew toy.

…about what I will be when I grow up, but it makes me very tired.

<u>Girls</u>

…my parents have no confidence in me.

…we are all living in someone's dream and that person could wake up at any time and we would disappear.

…that no one cares about me.

…about being old.

…that sometimes life goes by too fast.

…the world needs help—it's one big mess!

…I'm not good enough for anybody, but I am!

…that being a girl is not so easy.

…that my dad is going to come back.

…that I need to be more confident about my body, but still lose some weight.

…I'm the stupidest person in the whole world.

…how the world has changed because of guns.

…people just use me.

…no one believes I can become whatever I want. I plan on proving them wrong.

…why was I born—I don't think there's a reason for me to be living.

…deeply and beyond my normal feelings.

…that the world is just about money.

…the world really has problems when it's a big thing just to say hi or smile at a stranger.

SOMETIMES I THINK

Exercise:

1. Sometimes I think I shouldn't think so much! What are you thinking about that you could be acting on? You could start doing some research, make that phone call, check the Internet, apologize, give notice, or make the appointment—just start!

2. If you want to know what the youngster in your life is thinking about, create a safe place for him or her to open up. Go for a soda or ice cream or to the park or beach. The point is to make time for just the two of you and then try to relax and *be quiet*! This is not a time for the third degree, and don't be worried if conversation is almost nonexistent. If something heated does come up, resist launching into a lecture or passing judgment. Unless your opinion is asked for, brief comments like "wow," "I can imagine," "I bet," or "how great/awful" are non-threatening and appropriate. Be sure to thank the child for spending time with you.

God is...

Boys

...Buddha, and He's always watching over me.

...my Lord and Savior. He rules my life and loves me no matter what I do.

...to me more than a friend. Every time I need something, I tell him and he makes it happen. I try not to ask too often or for stuff I don't need.

...my helper, encourager, and Father.

...a Guardian of everybody.

...Someone who watches over me and tells me what is right or wrong.

...not much a part of my life.

Girls

...like my best friend. I pray to him every night. I really ♥ him.

...the One who loves me and always will.

...what I need in my life.

…my Heavenly Father that I can look up to and not be judged.

…someone you can't see but who is always there for you.

…my only reason for not doing certain things I could do.

…the person you turn to when nobody will listen.

…Buddha to my culture.

…my Guardian Angel.

…someone I look up to when I'm sad, mad, or just confused and someone I ask for advice.

…my diary. I tell him everything.

…my first priority and close personal friend.

…the music that pulls me out of my well of sadness and ocean of loneliness.

GOD IS

Exercise:

Is God or some other Higher Power a part of your life? If not, why not? Maybe you grew up with God as a cornerstone of your family. Do you recall this as being a great comfort, or did you resent being made to go to church? Perhaps you are one who sees God through nature and all living things, or you refer to God as Goddess, Spirit, or Higher Power. Do you feel your God has let you down or abandoned you? This is an opportunity to express your feelings about God or religion in general.

I dream of...

Boys

...working in the Air Force to support my family.

...nothing really—only nightmares.

...being rich and being poor because I don't think anyone should be treated differently because of how much money they have.

...going to places far out of this universe.

...having the girl in my dreams.

...the world being a better place.

Girls

...fantasies and things that could never come true.

...being someone else.

...how my life will be in the future.

...a peaceful and friendly world.

…being a bird and flying away.

…a better, more advanced Earth in the future.

I DREAM OF

Exercise:

Write about a dream you remember. If you don't recall a particular dream, create one! Write about how your life might be in
five or ten years, and include where you'll live and what kind of
home you will have. Do you see yourself traveling, working, or
volunteering? Who else is in the picture with you? Remember
that, for now, this is a dream, so make it a good one! It's amaz-
ing how positive thoughts can set positive events into motion.

When I'm alone, I...

Boys

...think of my mom and dad and me and my little sister all being together again.

...go to my parents' room and put my face in their pillows.

...think about my life.

...go crazy and start screaming.

...feel cold and lonely.

...feel sad because I remember a lot of things.

...do a bunch of stuff I don't get away with when my parents are around.

...love to sing and go on the Internet.

...feel I can cool down if I've gotten in trouble.

...read a book because it's quiet and peaceful.

...like to sit and think about what's going to happen next in my life.

…have thoughts that travel to the farthest places.

…have a tendency to cry or feel like I haven't made any friends.

…am scared because I live in a bad neighborhood.

…hug my pillow.

Girls

…turn up my music and make up dances.

…dream of an open field and flowers as far as I can see.

…like to draw or color or sit outside and watch the birds and clouds and think.

…like to read mystery books and not be disturbed.

…think about how good I have it and how much I have going for me despite all that's been painful in my life.

…think about the world's troubles and all the problems I have in my own life.

…read and write and imagine my future.

…fantasize about acting and being the center of attention. Being a romantic at heart, I also fantasize about the perfect relationship.

…wish there was someone beside me.

…think too much.

…feel like there's no one to turn to or get help from. I feel really helpless most of the time.

…think deep thoughts.

WHEN I'M ALONE, I

Exercise:

Alone time is when we have a chance to slow down and put our lives in perspective. It's a time to examine our priorities, set goals, or merely enjoy a well-deserved time-out. If you live alone, it's probably just a matter of re-arranging your routine. If you do not live alone, finding this time may not be quite so easy. But it's vital to your sanity to create some time just for yourself on a regular basis. It may be only an hour twice a week, when you lock yourself in your bedroom, put out a "Do Not Disturb" sign, and read, write, sleep, or whatever feels good at the time. Just do *not* be available. You may have to train your family to respect your space, but they will learn that when you emerge from your cocoon, you will be a more pleasant, peaceful, patient person. If you can take yourself to a movie, go for a drive, or walk on the beach, *do it*! Imagine the possibilities! Escape into you! You *are* worth it!

Oh, how I wish…

Boys

…we could have world peace.

…that my life could be better.

…that I could live with both my parents at once.

…that my brother was still alive.

…that I was much older and someone's Prince Charming.

…that people were more well-mannered.

…that my mom and dad weren't divorced.

…that I was a bird so I could fly away from my fears.

Girls

…my mom and dad were together again.

…I could feel better about myself.

…I had someone to share my hopes and dreams with.

…my life would be so much easier. I get a lot of peer pressure and I'm so tired.

…my family would become a family again and we could fill in the missing puzzle pieces that have been lost for so long.

…I don't wish. I try not to wish because it just gets my hopes up.

…that my room could stay clean. Every day I clean it, and somehow, by the end of the day, it's messy again.

…that my mom would listen to what I have to say.

…that the weekend could be longer.

…my parents would get back together so I wouldn't always have to be missing one of them.

…that my mom was still alive.

OH, HOW I WISH

Exercise:

There are many ways to make a wish. We wish on the first star we see at night, we make a wish as we blow out the candles on the cake, and we toss coins in a fountain. But most of us don't really express our longings. Years can go by and our dreams remain fantasies.

Writing about them with as much detail as possible can make your dreams and wishes seem more real, but a picture breathes life into your heart's desire. Begin by cutting out images from magazines that portray parts of your dream. Glue the pictures and words on a poster board, and perhaps even decorate the edges. Then place it where you can see it often. By visualizing yourself as part of your "treasure map," your dream may take on a life of its own. Or could you be afraid that your wishes might come true? What doors might you open that you may be afraid to walk through? You won't know until you step onto the path and allow positive thoughts to guide you.

I want to know

Boys

…what it would be like to be popular.

…how people could kill other people.

…where people go after they die.

…when my mom will be able to join our family here in the United States.

…what lies ahead for me.

…why woodpeckers don't get headaches, and if they do, why do they keep making holes in trees.

…what it's like to kiss a girl—I mean really *kiss*!

Girls

…who my real friends are and why there are cliques.

…everything about everything—like God!

…if I will remember anything when I die.

…why some people are racist and why some people still smoke when they know it will ruin their lives.

…more about my ancestors.

…why there seems to be more and more violence going on.

…who my husband will be.

…why boys were put on this earth.

…why some people think that because I'm small, I can't make a difference in this world.

I WANT TO KNOW

Exercise:

It's a good bet there's a question or two that's been on your mind for some time. I'm always wondering where I'll retire. I love both the ocean and the mountains, so I'm curious where my path will take me.

If you have a burning question, here is a process that may bring you some clarity. First sit comfortably and concentrate on your breathing until your "mind chatter" quiets down. This may be the hardest part! Ask your question, either out loud or to yourself, and then listen—just be still and listen. It may take some practice, but your inner voice, your "natural knowing" will likely answer you loud and clear.

If your question is one that can be researched, go to a library, attend a lecture, or take a class. If you have a child, you might even check the Internet together. Most youngsters are leaps ahead of adults on computers, and he or she would probably enjoy showing off his or her expertise.

If I were smarter I would...

Boys

...try to get better grades and not be put down all the time.

...help the homeless people get good jobs.

...have time to try out for more sports, because I always have a lot of hard homework.

...get a full scholarship to Harvard.

...find a cure for AIDS.

Girls

...find a cure for a broken heart, but I already know what it is..._love._

...think before I do so I wouldn't get in trouble as much. I'd learn from my mistakes.

...feel more confident about myself and not worry so much about school.

...tutor kids that need help, because I really like explaining things. It helps me understand more.

…have a lot of options in my life.

…find a way to bring my family closer together.

…be a mentor for kids that are on drugs or that have low grades.

IF I WERE SMARTER, I WOULD

Exercise:

Personally, the first response that comes to my mind is about learning from my mistakes. This probably is an ongoing challenge for many of us. But in examining the children's responses, I found it interesting that most seventh and eighth graders didn't equate intelligence with making a lot of money. Most of their answers dealt with being able to help others or to improve the world. I wonder at what point their altruism gives way to thoughts of financial gain. Certainly they get a glimpse of reality when their wants and needs exceed their allowance! But when does having a mansion or a Mercedes become more important than feeling good about what you do with your life?

I would say that if I were smarter, I'd find a way for people in the helping professions to be paid higher salaries for the important contributions they make to society. Otherwise, many young people are not going to pursue those careers.

Your turn: What would you do if you were smarter?

I'm proud of...

Boys

...myself and all my accomplishments.

...my sense of humor.

...my family and all they've achieved.

...all the good decisions I've made.

...having a father who served twenty years in the Army and fought in Vietnam.

...my mom for always being there for me.

Girls

...my one true friend. She has come so far in her life.

...being a vegetarian and working hard to achieve my goals.

...my mom and dad and how hard they've worked to get where they are.

...how I've grown to deal and cope with my life.

...myself, because I had a hard time in school and I've set a goal to get better grades and speak up.

...my sister and the way she's worked through her problems.

...the fact that I'm multiracial.

...myself, for simply being me. My life has not been uneventful, but I've gotten through it without too much pain.

...my personality and my ability to make people laugh.

I'M PROUD OF

Exercise:

1. Write about what you are proud of. This can be something you have worked long and hard to achieve, something you accomplished as a child, an award you've won, or something as simple as the fact that you do the best you can (on most days). Don't think about it too much. Just write whatever comes to mind. It's important to see it in print.

2. Tell your youngster, or your mom, dad, spouse, sibling, or friend something about them that you are proud of.

3. Tell them something else you're proud of again tomorrow. We all enjoy hearing good things about ourselves, even if we don't admit it, and it's difficult to be angry with someone who has just given us a compliment!

Three

So Many Emotions

I get mad when...

Boys

...I see people being bullied and picked on.

...people tease me.

...I work to my full ability and still don't accomplish my goals.

...I do my best and it's not good enough for my parents.

...my parents fight.

...teachers put me down in front of the whole class.

...adults don't think I have anything important to say.

Girls

...I get treated like a dog and ordered around.

...I have problems and no one listens.

...my brother hurts me and makes me cry.

...people talk behind my back.

...I get blamed because my brother lies to my parents, and they always believe the boys.

...I see people throwing their lives away on drugs and alcohol.

...people come up to me and put me down to my face, and, truthfully, I'm not going to just stand there and do nothing. I'll tell them they're acting stupid and I never want to talk to them again.

...girls follow me around and try to get me to fight.

...we have to follow the stupid dress code.

I GET MAD WHEN

Exercise:

1. Children need healthy ways to express their anger. Physical activities such as sports or martial arts are excellent outlets for frustration, and they certainly relieve more anxiety than most video games. Can your children safely show their anger around you without fear of retaliation? Talk with them about how important it is not to hold anger in, because they could wind up expressing it in inappropriate ways.

2. Think about your own anger buttons. The Serenity Prayer might help you make some conscious choices regarding people, places, and circumstances that upset you:

> God grant me the *Serenity* to accept the things
> I cannot change,
> The *Courage* to change the things I can,
> And the *Wisdom* to know the difference.
>   Reinhold Niebuhr

I feel like…

Boys

…I'm a good kid, because I'm helpful.

…I can do anything, if I just believe in myself.

…expressing my thoughts and desires to my friend, but I can't.

…a young child and that I should stay young for as long as possible, because we are grown-up for a very long time.

…I'm in a rut. The same thing, day after day.

…I've done many things to hurt other people.

…I'm in control of my life and my future.

…I need more support and help.

…I'm missing a great part of my life because of the World Trade Center tragedy.

…the sun…all warm inside.

…I can make a difference in the world.

…the world is my home and I love it.

…a geek with a little cool stuff in me, so it's a mixed feeling.

Girls

…I can do anything I want.

…I am falling behind in life and in grades.

…I'm the best that I can be.

…pointing out every wrong, stupid, mean thing about everything and fixing it.

…I want to cry when I see people getting hurt.

…I'm not good enough for certain people or things and I feel like screaming or yelling, sometimes.

…my mother is ashamed of me. She's always comparing me to her friends' kids.

…people hate me.

…there is something missing in me.

…an ant, compared to the Earth and the universe.

…a lot of people depend on me to succeed in life because I have big dreams.

…I can change the world. I'm the future and I plan to make the best of it.

I FEEL LIKE

Exercise:

Do you describe yourself with more negative than positive words? Trace the origins of those self-perceptions. The people and circumstances have probably changed, and it may be time to paint a new picture. Don't be so hard on yourself. A person who procrastinates may be gathering energy or information to attack the project. An indecisive person may just be thinking things through. A bossy person is probably a good leader, and a shy person is usually a good listener. What stories are you telling about yourself? Rewrite your script. Jot down some ideas about this subject.

What makes me sad is...

Boys

...that I don't get to spend much time with my dad, because he's always working on "projects."

...how many people die lonely.

...when bad things happen to people in my life.

...all the fighting in the world.

...teenagers dying because of drugs and alcohol.

...seeing people homeless and hungry and wondering what it would be like to live that way.

...that my family is never there when I need them.

...seeing children and animals being abused.

...the fact that I'm not with both of my parents.

...how some kids make fun of old people, but they don't ever think that the person might have served in World War II and helped save this country.

Girls

…when someone in my family dies.

…when I hear on the news about so many girls being kidnapped and raped.

…when my sister fights with my mom and dad.

…when I remember the good times and how it used to be.

…when a boy asks me out, and when I say yes, he turns around and says, "Ha, ha, I fooled you."

…seeing my sister suffer from depression caused by my parents.

…thinking about so much poverty and problems in the world, especially in my home country.

…seeing people I love ruining their lives and then treating me badly.

…that the world feels like a big ball of hatred.

…hearing stories that involve tragedies in the lives of children.

…hearing my family argue about bills until my mom cries.

…when I see kids younger than myself growing up without a mom and dad.

…being put in the middle of things.

<u>WHAT MAKES ME SAD IS</u>

<u>Exercise:</u>

Sadness can take many forms. The word "sad" may refer to a deep depression or a passing feeling of melancholy. It may be helpful to acknowledge your sorrow and examine what it's about. If you can trace it to a particular event, ask yourself some questions: What might I have done differently? Did I really have any control over the outcome? What information might have changed things? What lesson can I learn?

Perhaps your sadness is in remembering a time gone by, a person you miss, a lost opportunity, or the state of the world in general. Journal about it or even allow yourself to have a good cry. Give your grief a certain amount of time, but then *get into action*! Move your body, exercise, get out of the house and out of yourself. Physically and mentally *let go*!

I love…

Boys

…to play sports on sunny days.

…to let my imagination run wild.

…my parents the most, because they gave me life.

…having my mom to myself like when I was little.

…GOD.

…how things are going right now.

…my brother and my mom.

…this certain girl…and I have for as long as I can remember.

Girls

…my mom.

…going to school, for some strange reason. I just don't know why.

…perfume that smells so nice.

…my sister, because she's my best friend.

…to go out with my friends, because when I'm around them, I feel so happy.

…shopping!

…to be around people who help others and try to make a difference in their lives.

…to make up dances and play with makeup.

…peace and quiet.

I LOVE

Exercise:

Most of us don't often stop to think about what we love. Take a minute or so right now to look around. While you're at it, relax your shoulders. Most of us spend a good deal of time with our shoulders up around our ears. Take a long, deep breath. Now then, if you are at home, notice what puts a smile on your face. Are there pictures of people you care deeply about? Do you see beautiful flowers on your table or outside your window? Is there a treasured memento of a special occasion? Is your faithful pet curled up nearby? Take a little more time to consider all the blessings in your life. Most are obvious, such as your children, your spouse, going to the beach, holidays, and weekends. Give some thought to the many gifts that we take for granted, such as our health, our friends, and our freedom.

List a few of the things you love and describe why each is important to you, even if it seems obvious. Here's an example:

> I love my son. It's exciting to listen to his plans and ideas. It's been a joy to watch him become independent and make good decisions. I love his philosophical outlook on life and his sense of humor. I'm very proud of him for making a good life for himself pretty much on his own.

I dislike...

Boys

...cigarettes and their bad smell that I'm not allowed to complain about.

...not having my grandpa around.

...the way kids treat me and call me names.

...people cursing at me and pushing me around.

...domestic abuse.

...opera—it's too long.

...how people can be cruel to others because they're different.

...the way things are going between my brother and my dad.

...when my brother beats me up and no one stops him.

...being in advanced classes, because people expect too much from me.

Girls

...how children are not important to most people. They say, "Oh, it's just a kid."

...racists and war. I think that everyone is equal, no matter what, and that people who go to war are *sometimes* idiots.

...alcoholics and brussels sprouts.

...when girls get kidnapped and raped. It happens way too often—it's scary.

...racism, because it's so wrong to judge people by color.

...most vegetables, all meat except fish and chicken, social studies, when people smoke, and I'm sure there's a lot more.

...self-centered people who torment those who are not as pretty or popular as they are.

...the way my family fights with each other.

...when disabled people are made fun of.

...people who are hypocritical, mean, conceited, and braggers. I usually dislike homework, too.

...snobs, plastic surgery, cliques, and my ugly chin.

...when my parents think I've done something wrong and they won't let me explain.

...bullies. They are just pathetic losers who put down and torment others just to feel more powerful.

I DISLIKE

Let's see, I dislike:
1. The way that children are victims of so many injustices
2. Having to be subjected to other people's cell-phone conversations
3. Having to get up when it's still dark outside
4. Spiders
5. Tailgaters

Call this a gripe page. Write down some of the things that irritate you. Then consider again the Serenity Prayer. All those aggravations drain you of energy and can spoil an otherwise perfectly good day. What can you do something about, and what can you practice letting go of?

When I wake up...

Boys

...I listen to music to get me started.

...my eyelids feel like there are rocks on them.

...I say, "Another day," and get on with it.

...I take a deep breath and inhale the new day.

...I'm so excited because a new day is born and it's going to be a good day.

...I like to play with my brother.

Girls

...I feel tired and look very scary.

...I always sing and dance around the house.

...I put a smile on my face, because I know it won't be long until I see how my day will turn out. Hopefully, it will be a good day.

...I give thanks for another day to live.

...I say good-bye to my dreams and remember how cruel the world is—but we have to go through it.

...I feel a love for life.

...I'm the happiest person in the world until my mom starts yelling at me.

...I try to get a glimpse of the colors of the new day—sunrise.

...every morning, I give my mom and dad a big hug for always being there for me.

WHEN I WAKE UP

Exercise:

1. Here's an easy exercise. When you wake up, take a minute to be grateful for the new day, and if you pray, ask for wisdom and safekeeping for yourself and your loved ones.

2. If you have a teen or preteen, bring him or her a surprise cup of hot chocolate. It will make both of you feel good.

3. Here's a great habit to start: Get up just a little earlier to enjoy some quiet time for yourself before the hectic day begins. Have a cup of tea or coffee, do some stretches, or wake up your brain with a crossword puzzle. Think of it this way: it's a good idea to warm up your engine before entering the fast lane.

I'm afraid of...

Boys

…being alone in the dark.

…bad people.

…my dad when he yells at me.

…going upstairs at my grandma's house, because she has a lot
of dolls and they scare me.

…losing all my friends when I need them the most.

…being called on by the teacher.

…people dying—even me.

…fish.

…growing up.

…S-E-X.

Girls

…my past affecting my future.

…being alone when I grow up.

…letting my mom and dad down.

…things I can't see, like demons and devils.

…the graveyard and going to funerals.

…gangs, murderers, rapists, and kidnappers.

…spiders, letting people down, and telling people exactly
what's on my mind.

…being put in a situation where I might be hurt.

…sharks, mean dogs, and dying unloved, although I'm pretty
sure my parents will always love me.

…becoming an adult.

…dying.

…the world coming to an end.

…the sick-minded, crazy, perverted men in the world.

…September 11 happening here.

…nothingness. I'm afraid of suddenly being nothing, feeling
nothing, thinking nothing, etc.

…my mom dying. I've thought on it for as long as I can bear. I
know I'll be positively heartbroken. It scares me to death.

I'M AFRAID OF

Exercise:

When I was a little girl, I was afraid of thunder and lightning and spiders. I confess that today, I'm still not exactly thrilled by those creepy, eight-legged things. (One of my favorite "toys" is a bug vacuum).

Write about a leap of faith you've taken despite your fears. What action did you take without knowing all the facts? Was it the right thing to do? Would you do it differently had you taken time to think about it?

I clearly recall accepting my current teaching position. It was offered as a long-term substitute job with no benefits and no guarantee of permanence. On my first day of school, I showed up with all my belongings packed in my car and no place to stay. As it turned out, I was offered a place to live by the end of the day. It was a huge leap of faith and one I have never regretted.

Four

My Regrets

I am sorry...

Boys

...for people who have hate in their hearts.

...for some of the things I have done.

...that I've been a mean person sometimes.

...that I can't do more for abused children.

...I ever hit my brother because one way or another I always get paid back.

...that my parents are not married.

...that not everyone has a family.

Girls

...my grandma died before I could see her again. I didn't get a chance to say good-bye.

...for all the rude names I've called my mom.

...that so many bad things happen in our society.

...for all the bad things I've done in my life.

…for when I disrespect my parents or hurt their feelings.

…for letting my parents down because they count on me to do my best and be good in school.

…that I stole from my brother and lied once. God, please forgive me.

…for being mean to my brothers and sisters (although they deserved it).

…I picked the quiet road in my life.

…for all those people that have nothing when we have more than enough and waste it.

…for all the unhappiness some of my friends have to suffer, and on top of that, no one even believes it.

…that I stole my best friend's boyfriend.

I AM SORRY

Exercise:

1. Do you have amends you need to make to someone? If you are unable to verbally apologize for whatever reason, write a letter explaining how you feel. You don't have to give the person the letter. Sometimes just the intention can bring closure to the issue.

2. Do you owe yourself an apology? Have you ever put yourself in a compromising or dangerous situation? Have you verbally abused yourself? Take this opportunity to write down ten things that you are proud of about yourself. Better yet, say them to yourself in a mirror. Record a few positive affirmations into a tape recorder. There's a lot of power in hearing your own voice say things like "I am a positive and powerful person" or "I am lovable and capable."

If I could only...

Boys

...feed all the hungry people in the world.

...change time, because I would change the time my parents got divorced.

...make people see that same-sex parents can do just as good a job at raising kids as traditional parents (probably sometimes better).

...be a kid for a long time and never grow up and die.

...get my mother and father to stop ignoring me.

...be heard when I talk.

...go back and erase all the bad things I've done.

...let people know that kids have a lot of important thoughts and stuff to talk about.

Girls

...get to see my grandparents that passed away.

...find my father. I could die and be happy.

…help my sister with her attitude so we could be closer.

…build a new relationship with my father so I could be more comfortable around him.

…get a job and help my mom pay the bills.

…make my sister stop disrespecting my parents.

…keep drugs off the street.

…remember what I was thinking when I was born.

…feel safe in my neighborhood.

…make grown-ups know that not all teens think only of themselves.

IF I COULD ONLY

Exercise:

This thought is immensely personal. We all harbor many long-ings. Maybe it's to relive a special time gone by or to spend time with a lost love or a family member who has passed on. Perhaps there are angry words you'd like to take back or a different road you might have traveled. Maybe what you desire has more to do with your future. Complete the sentence with one or two of your own private dreams.

    If I could only _____

_____

_____

_____

_____

_____

I miss...

Boys

...the smell of my grandpa and grandma.

...my dog and my grandpa because they were important parts of my life.

...my mom.

...all the good times.

...the way my mom and dad used to get along.

...my mom who lives in the Philippines.

...all my friends from my old school. I wish they were here by my side.

...my dad. He's not dead, but I feel I don't get enough time with him.

Girls

...being able to talk to instead of argue with my sister.

...my dad...a lot!

...how it was only me and my mom and dad, but since my little sister came, they just yell at me.

...the way my family used to be.

...my best friend Jennifer who is in foster care.

...the 90s.

...the days when I was a little girl and my mom always talked about how good I was, but not anymore.

...my friend Brian, who I thought of as a brother until he started hanging out with the wrong crowd.

...the way my grandpa used to read to me and my uncle told me jokes, and I played the piano with my godfather, but they've all died.

...being kissed, put to bed, and tucked in by my mom.

...having time to just be with my parents.

...my mom, because I never lived with her, just my grandparents all my life.

...ignorance! I know so much now and I'm responsible for what I say and do.

...the friendship I had with my sixth-grade teacher.

I MISS

We all have times in our lives that we recall fondly. Some of these periods lasted a week or less, some a year or more. Think of a time that was especially significant for you. Close your eyes and travel back to that time. Allow yourself to have a full experience of it. What was the weather like? Did you spend your days in the comfort and warmth of a home, or was it an outdoor time? What smells were prevalent...freshly mown grass, cookies baking in the oven, hotdogs on the grill, your mother's perfume, or just fresh air? Was there bright sunshine or was it foggy and gray? What did you hear? Were there sounds of laughter, music, waves, birds, wind, rain, traffic, or sweet silence? Who was with you? Was it a parent or a special friend, lots of friends, or your children? Did you feel something you especially enjoyed, such as the warmth of flannel or the heat of the sun, grass, or sand beneath your feet?

Even with everything that made this time so memorable, would you really want to relive it? Think before you answer this question. Few places were as idyllic as we remember them, but I hope you had a wonderful visit. Time to return to the present and get busy making tomorrow's memories.

I used to love to...

<u>Boys</u>

...go fishing on weekends, but now my dad's too busy.

...hide under the blankets where no one could find me.

...do all kinds of sports, but now I don't have the time or equipment.

...run wild and just have fun being a kid.

...write poetry, but now I just get bored.

...play pat-a-cake.

...wait for the ice-cream truck.

<u>Girls</u>

...miss school, now I love school.

...sing my heart out.

...spend time with my family and relax, but now everybody is too busy.

...sing and do ballet. I was able to let my spirit free and show what I was capable of.

...stay home, but now I get bored and angry.

...spend time with my mom, because she would spoil me and play with me, but now she just yells at me.

...walk on beams and ledges, but since I fell, I don't find it too amusing.

...enjoy my free time, but now I don't have any. I miss being a kid.

I USED TO LOVE TO

Exercise:

Can you remember what you used to love to do? When did you stop singing in the shower, riding a bike, or shooting hoops? When did you last build a sand castle, take a nap, or swing in the park? We did those things to escape from reality and responsibility. With pressures today coming at us from many directions, it is even more vital to find your escape. If you used to play tennis, you could sign up for a class offered by the local parks and recreation department. Ask your child to join you in a game of old-fashioned chess, checkers, or Monopoly, or toss a ball around for a while. Maybe you could try something new, like kayaking or fencing. It doesn't matter what the diversion is—just *play*! You owe it to yourself!

Five

Ambitions

I try to...

Boys

...imagine that I'm the best football player in the whole school.

...put a lot of effort in everything I do.

...do my best, but I get distracted and end up getting in trouble.

...be a trustworthy kid.

...do my best to make my parents happy.

...focus on the good things in life.

...be nice to my brothers, even in hard times.

Girls

...be myself, but it's hard when I don't know who I am.

...be trustworthy, honor my parents, and be a good friend.

...live up to my parents' expectations.

...not put other people down.

…do the best I can, even though it may not look like it.

…make the best of my life so I don't regret anything that happened in the past (even though I already do).

…do my best in whatever challenge happens to come up.

…ignore the people who torment me when I'm awake and even in my dreams.

I TRY TO

Exercise:

Can you really "try" to do something? My sister always said,
"Trying is lying." Personally, I don't believe that, because if you
are making an effort toward a goal, you are in the process of
making it happen. Perhaps you're far from accomplishing the
goal, but it is progress.

What are you "trying" to do these days? Do you want to spend
more time with your children, eat a more healthy diet, work
fewer hours, or simply be a kinder person? Make a short list of
self-improvements you've thought about. For each, find one
simple action you could take toward reaching that goal.

Someday I will...

Boys

...see people learn to share this world and treat it with respect, because it's the only home we have.

...go to heaven and live eternally.

...have a good family and raise good children.

...invent a nonpolluting power plant that will help the environment, not harm it.

...play football with the greatest in the NFL.

...be successful and proud of myself.

...go very far.

...be a member of the Air Force.

Girls

...be a parent and respect what my child says, think about it, and take it seriously.

...live to see people learn how to make the world a safe, peaceful home, not a scary, violent place.

…live out my dreams.

…take my parents on a wonderful vacation.

…be like my teachers.

…stand on my own two feet.

…be a famous actress or model, because I'm willing to work hard to reach my goals.

…be really old!

…get away from all this pain and begin a new life for myself.

…prove to my mother that I can live a successful life. Right now she thinks I'll never make it on my own unless I "shape up."

…be the greatest athlete in the world.

…actually please my dad.

…be a marine biologist and invent a device that will allow people to go deeper in the water than they've ever gone before.

…be a parent and tell my children that I'll always support them through good times and bad.

SOMEDAY I WILL

Exercise:

How often have you said, "Someday I will have, do, or be _____"? Fill in the blank. How many "somedays" have come and gone? Wake up! This isn't a dress rehearsal and today turns too quickly into tomorrow. What can you do today that will get you even a little closer to that dream? Visit the place where you've considered moving or retiring. Join a gym. Sign up for that class. Give notice at your dead-end job. It's no news that if nothing changes—*nothing changes*!

Answer the following questions:

1. One goal I have is_____

_____

2. A step toward reaching that goal I can take immediately (OK, at least this week) is_____

_____

I want to see...

Boys

...my mom again in the future.

...my friends get the best out of their lives.

...my dad.

Girls

...all my friends together again.

...more peace and happiness in this crazy world.

...boys like me for just who I am.

...people get a clue.

...my little brother and sister grow up to be good, successful adults.

...my whole family in India.

...my aunts, uncles, and grandparents in Vietnam.

...a world without hate or violence, where there is no racism or pain.

…what it would be like to actually have somebody listen to what I have to say.

I WANT TO SEE

Exercise:

When I explain this thought, I suggest to my students that this might be about how their lives will look in the future. That could involve where they would be living or perhaps the career they'd be involved in. I suggest that it could describe a place they want to visit or something they want to accomplish at some point in their lives. I open the door to a variety of directions they could go with their answers.

So what do you want to see? Would you like to consult a crystal ball to find out when you'll retire, or whether you'll change careers or marry (again)? Do you want to see everyone in your family getting along? Do you want to see your hometown again and the street you grew up on? Do you want to visit Spain or Italy? Complete the sentence, and don't frustrate yourself trying to limit your response to one answer. I'm sure there's a world of things you'd like to see.

If I were older…

Boys

…I would have more freedom but more responsibility.

…I would be a better man and a friend.

…I would explore the world and the people in it and meet new faces.

…I would get a job and help my parents.

…I would go on lots of dates like my brother. He thinks he's so cool.

…I would probably understand better why my parents do the things they have to do.

…I'd have to pay taxes. It would be funny if I had to pay taxes on my allowance.

Girls

…I would buy a house and have my parents live with me.

…I would teach people far away about God and salvation.

…I would help raise my sister.

…I would work with the mentally handicapped and show them that they are capable of many things.

…I would drive to Southern California to visit my favorite aunt and uncle and take them to the beach for the day.

…I would help my parents with their frustrations.

…I'd be working on my goal of becoming a pediatrician.

…I would do whatever I want—mature things, that is.

…I would see all the R-rated movies I've missed.

…I'd want to take care of my parents and not put them in an elderly home, because they are full of wisdom that my children and I won't have.

IF I WERE OLDER

Exercise:

This could be wonderful food for thought and possibly a push to get your own life energized in a new direction. You know, you're not really stuck unless you insist you are. Demand limitations and they will surely be yours!

I love the idea that you could be reading this as a twenty-year-old or as an eighty-year-old and that there can be joy, excitement, and challenge ahead for each of us. Do you need to grow up and get a little more serious about how you do life? It's more likely you've been too responsible and you need to learn to play a little—maybe eat more ice cream and go barefoot more often. No matter what your age, each day brings an opportunity for new beginnings.

A Touch of Humor and Mythconceptions

Through the years I've collected some of the humorous comments that my students made with innocent sincerity. I hope these will make you smile.

- I asked a young man why he was flipping through career information cards. He replied, "I'm looking for a job that pays by the week or month. These all say per year, and I can't wait that long for a paycheck."

- If someone is autopsied when they die, does RIP mean "rest in pieces"?

- Miss Perry? Are we mature enough to watch the video about the girl who gets pregnant? It's been two weeks and I feel a lot more mature.

- One boy sagely advised the girls to take an auto mechanics class so they would know what the car repairman was talking about. A girl in class calmly responded, "That's why we get a husband!"

- I asked Jonathan why he was putting a piece of tape on his arm. He said it was a quit-swearing patch.

- In a paper about decision-making, Ralph wrote that the worst decision he made was when he was five and he thought his hamster could fly.

- For the same assignment, Tommy said his best decision was when he stood up to his brother. He also said it turned out to be his worst decision because his brother beat him up.

- Adults say we never take anything seriously. It only looks that way because the world is *very* serious today, and really, what are we supposed to do about it? The grown-ups made it the way it is!

- We are always being told we think we know everything. If we did, why do they make us go to school?

- My mom constantly yells about my room. Sure, it's a little messy, I *live* in it! It's not a movie set! If I wouldn't get in so much trouble, I'd ask her what *her* room looked like when she was thirteen.

- Adults always clump us into one big lump. They say, "You kids always blah, blah, blah." Then they tell *us* to respect everyone's individuality.

Epilogue

Although this book is about the world as seen through the eyes of middle-school youngsters, it is also about growing up at any age. The truth is that we all collect the puzzle pieces of our lives right up until that last odd little shape finds a home and our unique self-portraits are complete.

All adults who accompany children on their journey, whether by choice or by chance, must embrace the responsibilities and rewards of providing a firm foundation upon which children can build their lives. Talk to them, set boundaries, play fair, and be the solid role models they deserve. Know that they observe and absorb everything going on around them, and that imitation is not always the highest form of flattery.

Share thoughts, time, meals, hugs, and lots of laughter, all food for the soul. First and foremost, be the teachers your children need, more than the friend they think they want. Start today to create the wonderful memories you and your children can look back on when they are all grown-up. That day will be here all too soon.

Blessings to you and yours.

NOTES

NOTES

NOTES

978-0-595-36898-3
0-595-36898-0